HOW DID IT HAPPEN?
THE SECOND WORLD WAR

Cath Senker

FRANKLIN WATTS
LONDON•SYDNEY

First published in 2005 by
Franklin Watts
96 Leonard Street
London EC2A 4XD

Franklin Watts Australia
Level 17/207 Kent Street
Sydney
NSW 2000

Produced by Arcturus Publishing Ltd
26/27 Bickels Yard
151–153 Bermondsey Street
London SE1 3HA

Series concept: Alex Woolf
Editor: Philip de Ste. Croix
Designer: Stonecastle Graphics
Picture researcher: Thomas Mitchell
Maps: Encompass Graphics

Picture credits:
All the photographs in this book were supplied by
Getty Images and are reproduced here with their per-
mission. The photographs appearing on the pages
listed below are Time Life images.
Time Life Pictures/Getty Images: 17, 24, 25, 30, 43.

Every attempt has been made to clear copyright.
Should there be any inadvertent omission, please
apply to the publisher for rectification.

A CIP catalogue record for this book is available
from the British Library

ISBN 07496 5975 0

Printed in Singapore

Contents

1 What Were the Causes of War?

The Second World War was more widespread than any other in history. This devastating conflict involved 61 countries, which represented three-quarters of the world's population. The vast death toll included about 25 million deaths of military personnel and 25 million civilians. Millions more were left wounded and homeless.

There were three main areas of conflict: Europe, the Far East and the Pacific Ocean. The European war spread to envelop North Africa, and south-east Asian countries became involved in the Far East conflict. The war was fought on land in four major campaigns, at sea (in the Mediterranean, the Atlantic and the Pacific) and in the skies above the conflict zones.

Germany After the First World War

The conflicts of the Second World had some of their origins in the settlement after the First World War. After its defeat Germany suffered intense humiliation at the hands of the victorious Great Powers, led by France, Britain and the United States. Under the terms of the post-war Treaty of Versailles of 1919, Germany lost territory to France, Belgium, Denmark and Poland, and the coal-rich Saar region was taken over by the League of Nations. The treaty forced Germany to disarm its military forces and pay reparations to the victors for having started the war. In 1921 the amount was fixed at 132 billion gold marks – an enormous sum.

Germany also experienced political changes after the end of the First World War. In 1918, a democratic government that became known as the Weimar Republic was established. However, this government proved weak; it was threatened by both left-wing and right-wing organizations. In 1919, the left-wing Communists seized Berlin and other German cities during the Spartacist Rising, but the government managed to defeat them. Then in 1920 the right-wing anti-Communist Freikorps attempted to take power during a coup. The Weimar Republic withstood such threats but was clearly not a strong government.

In 1923 the strain of paying enormous war debts and reparations payments led to the collapse of the German economy. There was huge inflation and the German currency became worthless. It became common to exchange goods for food. In this German shop the sign reads 'Sales and repairs in exchange for food'.

Verkauf und Reparatur
im Tausch gegen
Lebensmittel

VOICES FROM THE PAST

'The disgraceful treaty'

The anger of the German people after the Treaty of Versailles is clearly expressed in this excerpt from the newspaper, the *Deutsche Zeitung*, in 1919:

'Today in ... Versailles the disgraceful Treaty is being signed. Do not forget it! The German people will with unceasing labour press forward to reconquer the place among nations to which it is entitled. Then will come vengeance for the shame of 1919.'

Quoted in Stewart Ross, *The Causes and Consequences of the Second World War* (Evans Brothers, 2003)

The Far East

Meanwhile in the Far East, conflict was brewing between Japan and China. Japan's government was heavily influenced by military figures who were intent on gaining control over neighbouring east Asian countries, including China. China was a country in turmoil. Since 1928, the Chinese government had been battling with the Communists, who wanted to take power in the country. Japan planned to take advantage of the instability in China to try to conquer Chinese territory.

The League of Nations

Under the terms of the Treaty of Versailles, an international organization was established to try to prevent aggression between countries, such as the Japanese threat to China, from leading to open warfare. Called the League of Nations, the organization adopted the principle of collective security. This meant that member countries agreed to act collectively against an aggressor, for example, by using economic sanctions, and to attempt to solve international disputes before they led to war.

This image from 1925 shows a cavalry patrol under the command of Chinese general Chiang Kai-shek riding through Canton, China. In 1928 Chiang Kai-shek established a national government, which was opposed by the Communist forces in the country.

In September 1931, Japanese forces attacked the Chinese garrison in Mukden in Manchuria, China. Over the next few months, the Japanese took control of the whole of Manchuria, which they turned into the puppet state of Manchukuo. Here, Japanese soldiers are seen entering Manchuria.

From the start, the League of Nations suffered from difficulties. It was supposed to represent all the countries of the world, but many powerful nations were not members: Germany was not allowed to join until 1926, the USA declined to become a member, and the USSR did not join until 1934. Japan and Germany then left the league in 1933, and Italy followed suit in 1937. Moreover, the league had no military force of its own. In 1923, Italy attacked the Greek island of Corfu, but the league took no action. In 1931, Japan began to carry out its plan to conquer territory in China, and overran the Chinese province of Manchuria. Again, the league did nothing.

The Great Depression
As international diplomacy failed, economic troubles caused another worldwide problem. In 1929, the Great Depression, a dramatic

economic collapse, hit the USA. Industrial production declined, many factories closed down and millions of workers lost their jobs. Short of money, the USA took back huge sums that it had loaned to other countries, such as Britain and Germany. There was a massive decline in international trade because the USA could no longer afford to buy large quantities of goods from other countries. This affected production in those places, and the Depression spread around the world. Between 1929 and the end of 1933, industrial production worldwide shrank by 40 percent.

These serious economic problems exacerbated political divisions in Europe, especially in unstable countries such as Germany and Spain. As unemployment and poverty increased, many people no longer trusted their governments. Some turned to extreme left-wing parties, and there was a dramatic rise in the popularity of Communism. Others turned instead to extreme right-wing political parties.

This photograph from 29 October 1929 shows workers pouring out onto the streets in New York City following the collapse in share prices that became known as the Great Crash. The collapse meant that the savings of many thousands of people became virtually worthless overnight. The stock market did not recover, and the US economy went into a deep depression.

VOICES FROM THE PAST

Living through the Depression

Millions of people lost their jobs and livelihood in the American Depression; the woman who wrote this testimonial was one of the luckier ones:

'In 1929 Orlo and I had been married two years and had a year-old son, Douglas. We were just nicely getting started in the turkey raising business on his parents' farm near Bridgeton. ... But that year was different. The newspapers were full of news about banks closing, businesses failing, and people out of work. There was just no money and we could not sell the turkeys. So we were in debt with no way out. ... But when we read about the bread lines and soup kitchens in the cities, we felt we were lucky because we raised our own food.'

Carmen Carter, *Michigan History Magazine*, January-February 1982 (Vol. 66, No. 1)

TURNING POINT

Hitler's rise to power

In elections under the Weimar Republic, each party gained seats in the *Reichstag* (parliament) in proportion to the number of votes it received – a system of proportional representation. Parties with similar policies could create a coalition to form the government. In the November 1932 elections, the Nazis won 196 seats and the Communists gained 100. The moderate left-wing SPD (Social Democrats) won 121 seats. If the Communists and SPD had formed a coalition, they would have had more seats than the Nazis and could have established the government. But they did not. The largest party was the Nazi Party, and in January 1933, President Paul von Hindenburg appointed Hitler as chancellor of Germany. Hitler's rise to power made war more likely.

Adolf Hitler's Nazi Party organized large rallies around Germany to demonstrate its strength and to attract people to the Nazi cause. At this rally in Dortmund in 1933, Hitler speaks to a crowd of Stormtroopers, an armed group founded by the Nazi leader that acted violently against rival organizations and helped to suppress resistance to the Nazis.

In Spain and Germany support grew for the extreme right-wing ideology of fascism (Italy had had a fascist government since 1922). Fascists believed in rule by one strong leader and thought that their nation was superior to others. They were prepared to use force against

enemies in their country and to conquer other nations. The form of fascism in Germany was Nazism; the Nazi Party's ideology incorporated the belief that the Jews were to blame for the country's problems.

The threat of fascism to world peace soon became clear. In Germany, the Nazi Party came to power in 1933. Its leader, Adolf Hitler, promised to seize back the German land lost under the Versailles Treaty of 1919 and conquer new lands to make Germany a great power. Italy's fascist government, led by Benito Mussolini, likewise sought to expand Italy's territory. Having already taken Corfu in 1923, Mussolini attacked Abyssinia (modern-day Ethiopia) in 1935.

With aggression among countries on the rise, European nations rearmed in the belief that war was likely. In Germany, Britain and France, serious rearmament began in 1936. According to the Treaty of Versailles, Germany's army was limited and it was not allowed to have an air force, submarines or large battleships. However, Germany rearmed secretly. In 1936, Britain started to develop new fighter aircraft, and the government introduced conscription in early 1939. France increased its military expenditure tenfold between 1934 and 1939.

The Sino–Japanese War

The tensions in East Asia led to conflict before they did so in Europe. In 1937 war broke out between Japan and China. Japan seized the major cities of Tianjin, Beijing, Nanking and Shanghai. It became clear that Japan aimed to acquire further territories in south-east Asia. This would potentially draw European countries into the dispute; Britain and France had colonies in the region, which Japanese expansion would undoubtedly threaten. The USA also had commercial and strategic interests there.

As open warfare erupted in the Far East, war was also becoming more likely to break out in Europe. Hitler began his campaign to expand Germany's territory. In 1936 his troops reoccupied the Rhineland on the border with France.

German troops and armoured vehicles parade through Vienna, the capital of Austria, during the German occupation of the country in 1938. There was no fighting; many Austrians at the time welcomed their country's incorporation into Germany. Hitler's move marked the first time since the First World War that a European power had crossed a frontier and imposed a territorial change through force.

This area had been declared a demilitarized zone according to the Treaty of Versailles. There was no opposition from the international community. Emboldened by this success, in March 1938 Hitler incorporated Austria into Germany, again in defiance of the Treaty of

Versailles. He then claimed that the Sudetenland region in western Czechoslovakia should be handed over to Germany because more than three million German-speaking citizens lived there.

Since the early 1930s, the British government had followed a policy of appeasement in response to Hitler's actions. In 1938, British prime minister Neville Chamberlain accepted Hitler's annexation of Austria. Then he met with Hitler and they concluded the Munich Agreement of September 1938, under which Czechoslovakia had to give up the Sudetenland to Germany. Chamberlain hoped that giving in to Hitler's territorial demands in the Sudetenland would prevent Germany from making further land claims. Hitler indeed stated that the Sudetenland was his final European land claim.

The British prime minister Neville Chamberlain (left) flew to Munich, Germany, to meet Hitler in September 1938. The French prime minister, Edouard Daladier, also attended the meeting. Neither Chamberlain nor Daladier consulted the Czechs about giving up the Sudetenland to Germany as part of the Munich Agreement. Both leaders returned to a hero's welcome in their countries; there were high hopes among the French and British populations that the Munich Agreement would prevent war.

Declaration of War

However, Hitler had no intention of halting his territorial advances. In March 1939, Nazi forces occupied the whole of Czechoslovakia, and Hitler drew up plans to attack Poland. In May he secured a full political and military alliance called the Pact of Steel with Italy. In August Hitler signed a non-aggression pact with the Soviet Union; the two countries agreed not to attack each other, nor to support any other party that might attack one of them. The USSR was Germany's enemy, and both sides knew that this pact was merely a temporary measure to postpone war between them. It made sense to Hitler because it meant he could attack Poland, which bordered the USSR, without the intervention of the Soviet Union. It was useful to the USSR too, because the country was unprepared for war, and because it had its own plans to take over Polish territory.

In August, Hitler made his move on Poland. He declared that he wanted to take over the Polish city of Danzig in the Baltic. Britain, Poland's ally, and France tried to persuade Poland to accept Hitler's demands, but the Poles refused. On 1 September Hitler invaded Poland. He thought the Western powers would not intervene, but this time he was wrong. The allied countries, Britain and France, declared war on Germany.

HOW DID IT HAPPEN?

Did Hitler start the war?

Until the early 1960s, most historians agreed that Hitler caused the war. In 1961, British historian A. J. P. Taylor challenged the theory: he claimed that Hitler did not want a world war but hoped to make a series of small territorial gains. The real reason for conflict was that countries such as Germany and Japan wanted to expand their power in the world. The long-established powers, mainly France and Britain, which already possessed many colonies and economic interests across the globe, wanted to stop them. In contrast, after making an exhaustive study of German documents, US history professor Gerhard Weinberg concluded that Hitler had indeed been determined to go to war 'and hoped to conquer the entire world'.

A. J. P. Taylor, *The Second World War* (Hamish Hamilton, 1975); Gerhard Weinberg, *The Foreign Policy of Hitler's Germany* (Humanities Press International, 1994)

German soldiers advance along a country road in Poland during the invasion of 1 September 1939. It was a rapid attack; German bombers attacked Polish communication lines and military strongpoints so that when German tanks advanced, they met with only weak resistance. In a series of bombing raids that followed, half of the Polish air force was destroyed.

2 European Powers at War

F or a few months after the declaration of war, there was what came to be known as a 'phoney war'. British and French leaders decided they could not intervene to save Poland. They did not perceive any sense of urgency in attacking Germany, as they believed that Germany had already overstretched itself and its economy would soon collapse. Britain and France set up war governments, with ministries of information, and an Allied Supreme Council was established to co-ordinate policies between the two countries. Yet they did not mount an attack on Germany.

While Britain and France remained inactive, in spring 1940 Hitler began a rapid advance on Europe, which became known as Blitzkrieg – lightning war. In April German troops occupied Denmark, which surrendered and remained under German control

This map shows the Nazi invasions of 1939 to 1941. As well as advancing through Europe and into the Soviet Union, in 1941 the Germans joined the Italians in their invasions of North Africa that had begun in 1940.

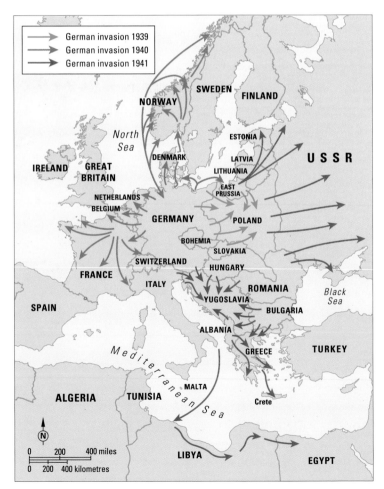

VOICES FROM THE PAST

'Victory at all costs'

Winston Churchill, who had opposed the policy of appeasement in the 1930s, became prime minister of Britain on 10 May 1940. Three days later, he made a speech to Parliament in which he said:

'I have nothing to offer but blood, toil, tears and sweat. … You ask, what is our policy? I will say: It is to wage war, by sea, land, and air, with all our might and with all the strength that God can give us. … You ask, What is our aim? I can answer in one word: Victory – victory at all costs, victory in spite of all terror; victory, however long and hard the road may be.'

Quoted in A. J. P. Taylor, *The Second World War* (Hamish Hamilton, 1975)

for the entire war. In May, the German army invaded Holland, Belgium and Luxembourg. The Dutch were overwhelmed within five days. Belgium and Luxembourg also fell quickly. By June Norway had fallen to the Nazis too.

The Germans launched an attack on France in May. The French resistance was feeble. Winston Churchill, the new British prime minister, promised assistance to the French. However, the British Expeditionary Force in France faced defeat by the Germans and its commander, General John Gort, decided to evacuate his troops rather than suffer enormous losses in France. He successfully evacuated them from Dunkirk, an event that the British people saw as a remarkable accomplishment. The French, however, were bitter at this withdrawal. Their own soldiers were left behind and the Germans captured them as prisoners of war.

The British Expeditionary Forces evacuate from Dunkirk, northern France in May–June 1940. The French were angry that they had been deserted by their allies. For them, the defence of their country was crucial, while the British were prepared to sacrifice France in order to preserve their forces to wage war elsewhere.

France Falls

In June 1940 the Germans completed their conquest of France. Hitler negotiated with the French leaders to divide up the country: northern France and the entire coast down to the border with Spain were to remain occupied by the Nazis, while France south of the Loire River would be ruled by a French government based at Vichy. This government, led by Marshal Philippe Pétain, collaborated with the Nazis; for every official measure, Pétain had to seek Nazi consent. Hitler had won domination over nearly all of Europe west of Soviet Russia within less than a year. At this point, Italy's leader Benito Mussolini scented victory. He declared war on the Allies and joined the conflict on Germany's side.

Hitler hoped that Britain would make peace and allow him to continue to pursue his aims in Europe. Britain would prove hard to defeat. Not only was it an island fortress but it was also a power in the Mediterranean; fighting Britain would mean sending German forces to North Africa.

Churchill, however, would not contemplate peace with Hitler, and thus Hitler planned for war. He knew that Germany's navy was far smaller than Britain's, so rather than risk a conflict at sea, he decided to bomb Britain's air defences in preparation for an invasion. From July to October 1940, the *Luftwaffe* (German air force) bombed British military targets such as harbours and airfields, along with factories and population centres, in an attempt to disrupt military production. In early September it looked as though the Germans were succeeding in grinding down Britain's defences.

However, Germany could not win a clear victory over the British air force. The Hurricane and Spitfire fighter aircraft of Britain's Royal Air Force (RAF) were able to destroy the German bombers. Britain had developed a radar system that warned RAF fighter pilots when bombers were approaching so they could engage them before the Germans attacked. Between 12 August and the end of September, the Luftwaffe lost over 1,773 aircraft while Britain lost 915. Hitler postponed his planned invasion of Britain indefinitely.

A British Hurricane fighter plane is refuelled in August 1940 at an RAF Fighter Station during the Battle of Britain. As well as having the benefit of radar that could identify the position of *Luftwaffe* aircraft, the RAF enjoyed other advantages over the Germans: the British air force was operating over home territory and could attack, land and refuel relatively easily.

Bombing Cities

Following the Battle of Britain, Germany turned to area-bombing British cities at night in a campaign that was commonly known as the Blitz. Between September 1940 and May 1941, German bombers

TURNING POINT

Failure of the Battle of Britain

The *Luftwaffe* failed in the Battle of Britain for various reasons. It simply did not have enough fighter planes for the task in hand. These were needed to escort the bombers on their missions and give them cover, and also to engage the British fighters. British Fighter Command had just enough aircraft to keep up the fight. This was achieved by the continual manufacture of new planes and the speedy repair of damaged ones. The Germans underestimated the strength of the RAF. Their failure in the Battle of Britain was a turning point because, without command of the skies, Germany could not successfully invade Britain.

Firefighters in the City of London put out a fire on 30 December 1940 after a bombing raid during the Blitz. The previous night, a massive German raid had sparked huge fires. Firefighters were forced to blow up buildings to create fire-breaks to stop the fire from spreading from street to street.

attacked railways, ports and city centres in an effort to disrupt communications and destroy morale. About 3.5 million homes were damaged or demolished, and around 43,000 people lost their lives. However, the bombing, which was often indiscriminate, did not seriously affect war production.

In return, British aircraft bombed German cities. There were insufficient fighter planes to provide cover for daytime bombing, which would have enabled the bombers to target vital industries, so the British also resorted to indiscriminate night-time bombing. This campaign ended in November 1941 when the Royal Air Force realized the bombing campaign was more costly to Britain in terms of air crew and production than it was to Germany.

Beginning in June 1940, Hitler adopted another tactic against Britain – blockade. This was an attempt to isolate the island nation by stopping the supply of goods by sea. Germany itself was well supplied with

goods from all over Nazi-occupied Europe and from its ally, the Soviet Union. In a campaign that became known as the Battle of the Atlantic, Germany used submarines called U-boats to attack British shipping in the Atlantic Ocean. At first this tactic was extremely successful. Between June and December 1940, U-boats sank over 3 million tonnes of Allied shipping, which meant a drastic reduction in supplies reaching Britain. Rationing had already been introduced in the country in January 1940, but in spring 1941 rations had to be reduced still further.

To combat the serious shipping losses, British vessels started to travel in convoys. The RAF patrolled the sea lanes to protect the vessels from attack. Help from the USA arrived; warships were supplied to patrol the western Atlantic. By autumn 1941 these warships were also sinking U-boats and had become a target themselves.

Axis Powers on the Offensive

While the Battle of the Atlantic was proceeding, Hitler decided to bolster his alliances with friendly countries. He initiated a Tripartite Pact between Japan, Italy and Germany, which was signed in September 1940. Under the pact, each country promised to enter into the war if any of the others was attacked by a new enemy.

A German U-boat surfaces in 1940. German code-breakers had figured out how to read British naval signals, and this helped them target British ships accurately. The U-boats frequently travelled together in packs to attack them. However, the submarines moved slowly and had to cover great distances under the ocean, so many British convoys were able to evade their pursuers.

Although Italy and Germany were allies, they pursued separate courses. Mussolini had so far been excluded from Hitler's war plans and he now initiated his own campaign without consulting his German ally. He aimed to expand Italy's territory just as Hitler had conquered lands in western Europe. In August 1940 Mussolini sent a force into Somaliland (modern Somalia and Djibouti), and the following month an Italian force entered Egypt. In October, Italian forces launched an attack on Greece and on Tobruk in north-eastern Libya.

These incursions threatened Britain's interests in the Mediterranean, where it had a fleet stationed. Britain also had an army in Egypt to protect the Suez Canal, a key element in the shipping route to its empire. Italy's offensive was unsuccessful. The British navy attacked the Italian navy at Taranto, Italy in November and recaptured Tobruk the following January.

The USA hoped to boost the Allies' war against the Axis powers, which had expanded geographically following Mussolini's invasions in Africa. In March 1941 the USA set up a new system to support the Allies. It instituted a lend-lease policy: Britain could place orders for American materials, which were paid for by the US government. The materials were leased to Britain, which promised to pay for them after the war. This economic backing gave the USA a powerful role in the conflict.

The theatre of war now expanded further in Europe and into the Middle East. In spring 1941 Hitler went to the aid of Italy in its failing campaigns in south-eastern Europe. Italy had invaded Greece in October 1940 but had failed to conquer the country.

German soldiers in the field compose coded messages on an Enigma enciphering machine. At their peak during wartime, the Germans used about 200 different Enigma keys, or codes, and all these keys were changed every 24 hours. The complexity of this system presented a considerable challenge to the British code-breakers who were attempting to crack the Enigma codes.

TURNING POINT

Decoding Enigma

In 1940 British intelligence first succeeded in breaking some of the Germans' top-secret codes that were created by the Enigma machines, which were used by all branches of the German armed services. The process of decoding of German secret codes was called Ultra. In May 1941, the British Royal Navy captured a German submarine with its Enigma machine and codebooks. From then onwards Allies could decode naval messages, which made a significant contribution to their intelligence operations during the Battle of the Atlantic. They were later able to break the codes of other elements of the German armed forces, such as the *Luftwaffe*. However, the Nazis also had success in this area. For example, by 1939, their specialists had already cracked British naval codes, and in February 1942 they deciphered the Allied code for communication with the convoys in the Atlantic.

German tanks move in convoy in Cyrenaica, Libya. A colony belonging to Libya since 1912, Cyrenaica became a major theatre of operations during the Second World War. The British occupied the area after the second Battle of El Alamein in October 1942.

German forces now took control of Greece and also of Crete and Yugoslavia.

In addition, the Nazis helped the Italians fight the British forces in an attempt to take control of British colonies in North Africa, and the conflict spread across North Africa to Syria, Lebanon and Iraq. In March 1941 Nazi general Erwin Rommel attacked Tripoli in Libya, and the following month his army entered Egypt. Germany threatened Syria, a French colony, but was defeated by French forces in June. Then in late June, the focus of attention moved abruptly away from the Middle East and back to Europe.

HOW DID IT HAPPEN?

Did Winston Churchill defend democracy?

British historian Professor Geoffrey Best argues that Churchill was a 'defender of democracy'. 'The normal peacetime freedoms of the citizen were of course restricted but rarely beyond the limits of reason. The world could see no hypocrisy in Churchill's claim to be fighting for democracy and human rights against tyranny and barbarism.'

However, left-wing historian Chris Harman argues that Churchill was indeed a hypocrite because he did not support democracy in other places, especially if they were British colonies. During the war Churchill said: 'I did not become his majesty's first minister in order to preside over the dissolution of the British Empire.' In 1942, the Quit India campaign against British rule in India was crushed by British forces.

Geoffrey Best, *'Winston Churchill: Defender of Democracy'*, BBC History website, 2002; Chris Harman, *A People's History of the World* (Bookmarks, 1999)

German soldiers advance through a burning village in Russia during Operation Barbarossa, the German invasion of the Soviet Union in June 1941. Russia had not taken precautions to guard itself against an attack in case such measures should provoke war with Germany. Mobilization of its armed forces for the defence of the country did not take place until several days after the start of the invasion.

Operation Barbarossa

Hitler's principal ambitions were not in North Africa but to the east of Germany. He intended to conquer the USSR to provide *Lebensraum* (living space) for the German people and to control its rich natural resources – especially oil. He thought the Soviet Union would prove an easy conquest. In June 1941 he launched Operation Barbarossa, an invasion of the Soviet Union. Hungary and Romania were drawn in on Germany's side, and the USSR became one of the Allies. Britain offered to help the Soviet Union with supplies, yet militarily the USSR was left to fight Hitler alone.

In August 1941, German forces advanced on Leningrad and began a siege of the city that lasted 900 days and caused around 600–800,000 civilian deaths. In September, they captured the Ukraine, most of the Crimea and the Donets basin. At the end of September, the Germans began to advance on the capital, Moscow, but were halted in the winter of 1941–42 due to the freezing cold and lack of resources.

3 An International Conflict

While the enormous struggle between Germany and the USSR was underway during the second half of 1941, the conflict in the Far East also grew in size and intensity. The Western powers had colonies in the region, which Japan now threatened. In late 1941 this brought them into the Far East war that Japan and China had been fighting since 1937.

Japan had plans to create a Japanese empire in Asia. Its rulers believed that the USA was preoccupied with Europe and as a consequence would permit Japan to expand its territory. This proved to be a miscalculation. The USA had business and strategic interests in the Pacific that it wanted to defend.

In July 1941, Japan moved its forces deep into the French colony of Indo-China. The USA responded by imposing an embargo to prevent the supply of oil to Japan. It froze Japanese assets, which meant that Japanese businesses in the USA could no longer operate. US president Franklin D. Roosevelt said these restrictions would be lifted only when Japan pulled its troops out of Indo-China and China.

Yet Japan had no intention of pulling out. On the contrary, on 7 December Japanese forces went on the offensive with a surprise

On 7 December 1941 Japanese aircraft attacked US warships at anchor in Pearl Harbor. Within two hours, the impressive naval base on Hawaii was reduced to a ruin with flaming warships ablaze in the water. The Americans had received evidence through intelligence sources and from their Allies that some form of Japanese attack was imminent but no effective counter-measures were taken.

TURNING POINT

The attack on Pearl Harbor

Tojo Hideki, who became Japanese prime minister in October 1941, believed in the supremacy of the Japanese people and keenly supported the alliance with Italy and Germany. He felt that war with the USA was bound to happen. The oil embargo would soon have a serious effect on the Japanese economy; the country was using nearly ten times as much oil as it could produce per year. Japan would either have to back down or fight the USA, and Japan did not want to abandon its ambition to create an empire in Asia. Japanese admiral Yamamoto Isoroku decided that a first strike against its enemy's naval fleet could stop the USA from thwarting Japan's expansion plans. However, the strike against Pearl Harbor was not the spectacular victory that Yamamoto hoped for, and the entry of the USA into the war led instead to the frustration of Japan's imperial plans.

Hong Kong was not adequately protected by the British and it fell easily to the Japanese in December 1941. Following the Japanese capture of the island from Britain, these British prisoners of war (POWs) are seen leaving Hong Kong to be transported to a Japanese prison camp. Conditions in Japanese camps were extremely harsh. By the time Japan surrendered in 1945, 27 percent of the POWs from Britain and the allied countries of the British Commonwealth and 37 percent of American POWs had died in captivity.

attack on Pearl Harbor, an important US naval base in Hawaii. They destroyed much of America's naval fleet; 2,403 US troops and 64 Japanese lost their lives. However, they failed to destroy the US's oil reserves in Hawaii and did not hit any aircraft carriers, which by chance were at sea on that day. Nevertheless, the attack led Britain and the USA immediately to declare war on Japan. Then Germany and Italy declared war on USA. World war had begun.

War in the Pacific

The Japanese forces moved rapidly to consolidate their advances, launching invasions of Malaya, Thailand and the Philippines the day after the attack on Pearl Harbor, and invading Burma just three days later. On 22 December they captured Manila, capital of the US-controlled Philippines, from American forces and on Christmas Day they took Hong Kong (an island near China) from the British – along with 12,000 prisoners of war. Churchill called this 'the worst disaster and largest capitulation in British history'.

This map shows the extent to which the Japanese Empire had expanded by 1941 and subsequent conquests by Japan following its entry into the Second World War. The Empire was at its largest in 1942, after which Japanese forces began to be pushed back towards their homeland as the Allies went on the counter-offensive.

By the end of 1941, Japan, Germany and Italy had all vastly increased their territory and for much of 1942, they continued their campaign of conquest. In the Far East, Japan rapidly expanded its acquisitions over a period of three months, and took over long-established colonies from the Western powers. One of these was the Philippines. There, US forces gave up the fight against the Japanese in late February, leaving the Filipinos to continue the resistance. By May the Philippines had surrendered to Japan.

Japanese forces continued their expansion into Malaya, Singapore, Borneo, Burma and the Dutch East Indies. By March 1942, the Japanese had conquered a wide swathe of territory from the borders of India to the borders of Australia, and far out into the Pacific Ocean, including the Solomon, Marshall and Mariana islands. The Australian government expanded its military forces in the fear that Japan might invade Australia.

Island Hopping

After March 1942, the USA achieved important victories against Japan, and Japan's southward advance began to lose momentum. The USA won the Battle of the Coral Sea (May) and the Battle of Midway (June). It adopted a strategy of 'island hopping' – moving eastwards island by island across the Pacific Ocean to take back islands from Japan. In August 1942 US Marines landed on Guadalcanal, one of the largest of the Solomon Islands. There was a six-month struggle on Guadalcanal, which was eventually won by the Americans in February 1943.

At the same time, Australian forces fought the Japanese in Papua in New Guinea, which the Japanese had invaded in July 1942. Australian forces fought a bitter counter-attack against them, which was finally successful in January 1943.

An image from the Battle of Midway in June 1942 shows the American aircraft carrier USS *Yorktown* under attack. The battle marked the first decisive defeat that Japan suffered at the hands of US forces. Japanese bombers flying from aircraft carriers launched the first strike against the island of Midway. On their return, Admiral Yamamoto ordered a second raid. While the Japanese planes were refuelling, US torpedo bombers flew in and sank all four of the Japanese aircraft carriers. The USA lost just one carrier, USS *Yorktown*.

TURNING POINT

!

Battle of Midway

Admiral Yamamoto Isoroku attacked the US-held islands of Midway as a step towards occupying Hawaii and so that they could be used as a base for an attack on the Pacific coast of America. He aimed to draw US aircraft carriers and ships into a battle and destroy American naval power by using an attack on the Aleutian Islands as a diversionary trick. Japan conquered the Aleutians but the strategy to attack Midway went disastrously wrong. The USA had intercepted Japanese naval codes and was aware of the plan. The Japanese navy had no radar for detecting enemy ships. Faulty intelligence meant its commanders underestimated the US forces on Midway. Within 24 hours, Japan lost all four of its largest aircraft carriers, 332 aircraft and 3,500 sailors. This battle marked a huge reversal in Japan's fortunes.

North African Battles

While battles raged in the Pacific, Germany was pursuing the war in North Africa. Like Japan in the Pacific, Germany experienced successes in the first part of 1942. In June German forces seized Tobruk from the British and advanced into Egypt. British commander General Sir Claude Auchinleck then checked the advance of the German and Italian forces at the Battle of El Alamein in July. Churchill urged a further attack to destroy the Axis forces in North Africa. He was under pressure from Soviet leader Joseph Stalin to begin an invasion of occupied Europe but wanted to complete the African campaign

British general Bernard Montgomery scans the horizon from the turret of a tank in Egypt during the North African campaign. During August 1942, Churchill put pressure on Montgomery to launch a renewed attack at El Alamein as quickly as possible, but Montgomery resisted Churchill's demands. He wanted first to build up his numbers of tanks, aircraft and men to achieve a decisive advantage over Rommel's German troops. He correctly informed Churchill that if the Allied forces waited until October, the attack would be successful.

VOICES FROM THE PAST

In defence of Montgomery

Harold Alexander was British commander-in-chief in the Middle East and worked closely with Montgomery at the second Battle of El Alamein. In his 1961 autobiography he defended Montgomery's actions in not completely destroying Rommel's army.

'At Alamein Rommel was utterly defeated but not annihilated: Alamein was a decisive victory but not a complete one. It is easy to look back after eighteen years and suggest that the Afrika Korps [German combat units in North Africa] could have been destroyed by a more vigorous exploitation after the breakthrough, but let us remember the realities of the time.

Monty had his first big command. He was new to the desert. He was fighting a great battlefield tactician in Rommel, whose troops were seasoned warriors: he and they had won some remarkable victories; whereas the Eighth Army had only recently been reformed and given the material to take on the Axis at better odds; many of our fresh reinforcements were new to desert conditions; and although our Intelligence was good we couldn't know accurately what punch the Germans were still nursing.'

Harold Alexander, *The Alexander Memoirs: 1940–45* (Cassell, 1962)

first. He now appointed General Bernard Montgomery to command the Eighth Army, which was to fight in Egypt.

In October Montgomery mounted his counter-attack against the Axis powers. His forces outnumbered the Germans and Italians by about two to one. Montgomery achieved victory at the second battle of El Alamein although he did not completely destroy Rommel's army.

Following this British victory, in November US and British forces launched an invasion of North-West Africa, with the aim of defeating German and Italian forces in the Mediterranean. They landed in French-controlled Morocco and Algeria; in response the Germans occupied southern France and Tunisia, which were also under French control. The Germans and Italians poured troops into Tunisia in December. Now their forces in North-West Africa outnumbered the US, British and French forces. The conflict in the region was not over yet.

A US task force travels towards North-West Africa to participate in Operation Torch, the Allied invasion of the region that took place in November 1942. At first, US military leaders favoured a landing in Europe, but by July 1942 they accepted the wisdom of this strategy.

At Nazi work camps such as Auschwitz in Poland, inmates were forced to work until they died of exhaustion. There was also a death camp at Auschwitz, called Birkenau, where Jews were deliberately murdered in gas chambers. These children pictured at Auschwitz in 1945 are some of the very few survivors; it is thought that over a million people died in Auschwitz-Birkenau.

HOW DID IT HAPPEN?

Was the Holocaust deliberately planned?

Some historians of the Holocaust, such as Lucy Dawidowicz, argue that the Holocaust was deliberately planned much earlier than the Wannsee Conference of 1942. Hitler had expressed his hatred of the Jews since 1919 and his plan had always been to annihilate them.

Other historians, such as Martin Broszat, argue that the policy to destroy the Jews arose in a piecemeal fashion as the Nazis gained greater control over Europe. The Nazis took advantage of the situation created by the war.

Steven R. Welch, *'A Survey of Interpretive Paradigms in Holocaust Studies and a Comment on the Dimensions of the Holocaust'* (Yale University, 2001)

Nazi Terror

As the war in Africa waged on, in Europe the Nazis were pursuing a vicious campaign against the Jews. Since gaining power in 1933, Hitler had stripped Jewish people of their rights and imprisoned many Jews in concentration camps. Beginning in the autumn of 1941, the Nazis deported Jews from Germany and German-occupied countries to ghettos in Poland. Also during 1941, death squads called *Einsatzgruppen* rounded up Jews, Roma people and Communists and murdered them. Hitler wanted to destroy the Jewish people once and for all. At the end of 1941, the Nazis started to build death camps where they could systematically murder their enemies.

This murder policy was formalized at the Wannsee Conference in January 1942, at which the Nazis decided on a 'Final Solution' to annihilate the Jews. They would deport all the European Jews to work camps and death camps in Poland. The fittest would be worked to death while the others would be killed immediately. Although Germany was fighting a world war, its leaders were prepared to use up vast amounts of resources in pursuit of this aim. They invested in sophisticated technology to create an organized system of murder and built gas chambers so they could kill thousands of Jews daily using poison gas. This attempt to wipe out an entire people became known as the Holocaust.

The siege of Stalingrad

In 1942, as the Nazi campaign against the Jews accelerated, the Germans also mounted a renewed offensive against the USSR. Hitler was determined to destroy Soviet military and economic power. The first aim was to capture Stalingrad and to seize the oilfields in the Caucasus to the south. In August, German forces besieged Stalingrad, which was fiercely defended by the Russians. Nazi General Paul Ludwig von Kleist, commander of the most southerly army, advanced towards the Caucasus, but when snow fell in October he could go no further and he never reached the main oilfields.

A woman worker welds in a German factory producing Messerschmitt aircraft. Germany brought in labourers from the countries it had occupied to work in its munitions factories. At the start of the war, volunteers and prisoners were used, but by 1941 foreign workers were being forced to labour in Nazi arms factories. The conditions for most foreign workers were appalling.

While troops fought on the ground in the Soviet Union, the air and sea wars between Britain and Germany were pursued with ferocity during 1942. The two air forces continued to attack each other's countries: the RAF bombed the German cities of Lübeck, Cologne and Hamburg, and the Luftwaffe bombed Exeter, Bath and other English cities. In the naval war, the Germans enjoyed some success in the Battle of the Atlantic: in early 1942 they had changed the Enigma code, so the Allies could not discover the whereabouts of German U-boats using Ultra intelligence. The USA, which had entered the Battle of the Atlantic on the Allies' side, had not introduced protective measures, such as travel in convoys, so it lost many surface ships. German U-boats succeeded in sinking nearly 500 Allied ships in the first half of 1942.

4 Allies on the Offensive

The year 1942 had been a pivotal one in the course of the war as the Allies began to fight back against the Axis powers. In January 1943, Churchill and Roosevelt met at the Casablanca conference, where they announced that 'unconditional surrender' by the Axis powers was the Allies' aim. At the time, the Soviet Union was desperate for a second front in the war against Germany to be established, for instance, by initiating an Allied invasion of northern France that would proceed to attack Germany. Such an incursion would force Germany to divide its forces and weaken Hitler's offensive against the USSR. Yet Britain and the USA did not plan to open a second front in 1943.

Nevertheless, the Allies made progress towards the defeat of the Axis powers during the year. The USSR had successes on the Eastern Front as its forces managed to hold out against the Nazis. Meanwhile, Japan and Germany suffered defeats in the Far East and North Africa respectively.

Germany's fortunes in the Battle of the Atlantic were also reversed during 1943. A turning point was reached in April. Improved anti-submarine tactics, better weapons and new technology enabled the Allies to sink greater numbers of U-boats. In March the Germans lost just one U-boat but in May they lost 41. Hitler then called off the battle. A total of around 75,000 to 85,0000 Allied seamen and around 9,000 U-boat seamen had died during the campaign.

A British soldier searches a German prisoner captured in Tunisia in 1943. When the Axis forces surrendered in May 1943, the Allies took more than 250,000 prisoners, including 125,000 German troops.

The Eastern Front

While Germany lost battles in the Atlantic, its aims in the east were thwarted too. In February 1943, Soviet forces defeated the Germans and their allies, the Romanian, Hungarian and Italian armies, at the Battle of Stalingrad. The first major defeat of Hitler's armies in the USSR, it represented a huge blow to German morale as well as a military defeat. The more significant battle, however, was the Battle of Kursk in July, in which the Soviet forces again defeated the Germans. The battles around Kursk cost Hitler half a million men and he could no longer avoid defeat in the east. Between August and

TURNING POINT

The Battle of Kursk

As the Soviet forces prepared for the Battle of Kursk, they were in a good position, with far more guns and soldiers and better tanks than the Germans; the USA provided trucks and food. On 5 July, the Germans attacked and a week later the Russians initiated a counter-offensive. There were 1,500 tanks engaged on each side – the biggest tank battle in history. The Russians were victorious. This decisive battle put an end to Hitler's dreams of conquering the Soviet Union and laid the way for the Soviet offensives of 1944-5.

German soldiers enter a bomb-damaged factory in the city of Stalingrad in 1942. The battle for Stalingrad was a major turning point in the war on the Eastern Front. The German Sixth Army under the command of General Friedrich Paulus was directed to seize the city. By October 1942 Paulus' troops had occupied about two-thirds of the city but Soviet forces then counter-attacked and succeeded in surrounding them. The fighting lasted for several weeks but finally, on 31 January 1943, Paulus surrendered. The Germans lost 200,000 men at Stalingrad, while 110,000 more were taken prisoner.

December, the Soviet forces advanced, extending the fighting along a wide front from the Baltic in the north to the Black Sea in the south.

The Soviet forces were not the only ones that achieved successes against Germany. In spring 1943, US and British forces fought Rommel's army in North Africa. By March, after his defeat at the Battle

British troops in Burma face Japanese machine-gun fire from across a river. In December 1942, the British were completely new to jungle warfare. They fought alongside Indian troops and Gurkhas (soldiers from the Nepalese force in the British army). In early 1943, General Harold Alexander decided that the defence of India was the priority and Burma would have to be abandoned. In May 1943 the Allied troops faced gruelling retreats on foot to the Indian border.

of Médenine, southern Tunisia, Rommel warned Hitler it was 'plain suicide' for the Axis forces to remain in North Africa. By mid-May the Allies had conquered Tunisia; the Axis forces in North Africa surrendered and the Allies were masters of the region.

While the North African campaign continued, in the Far East Japan was still in a strong position at the beginning of 1943. China was cut off from the Allies by the Japanese occupation of Burma. British forces had launched a land offensive in Burma in December 1942 in an attempt to defeat Japan and reopen the Burma road – the route between India and Chungking, the temporary capital of China. But the Japanese protected themselves in the mountains and rain forests, and the British were forced to withdraw in May 1943.

Battles in the Pacific

The tide began to turn against Japan elsewhere, however. In February 1943, Japan lost Guadalcanal and Papua, and could no longer extend its power southwards. Japan now concentrated on the defence of strategic points, especially New Guinea and the Solomon Islands. A US military conference in March 1943 called for counter-attacks against the Japanese to reconquer these regions. A key aim was the capture of the powerful Japanese naval base at Rabaul, where about 110,000 Japanese troops were based.

The USA continued the strategy of island hopping to reconquer territory from Japan. In May its soldiers recaptured the Aleutian Islands. The attack finished with the invasion of the island of Attu, where troops killed most of the 2,300 defenders.

In June the Americans began their attack on the Japanese forces in New Georgia and the Solomon Islands. US general Douglas MacArthur adopted a tactic of envelopment to break the lines of communication between the Japanese-held islands and isolate them from each other. Each Japanese-held island was able to communicate with the next island in the chain but was not able to communicate with more distant Japanese-held islands. Rather than attack a Japanese stronghold head on, MacArthur would instead attack the next, but smaller, Japanese-held island in the chain. This broke lines of communication between the two and isolated the stronghold.

VOICES FROM THE PAST

A brutal environment

Lieutenant-General R. L. Eichelberger, Commander of the 32nd US Army Division in Papua, described the fighting there:

'It was about one part fighting to three parts sheer misery of physical environment. It was climbing up one hill and down another, and then, when breath was short, fording streams with weapons held aloft or wading through swamps. It was sweat and then chill; it was a weariness of body and spirit; and once again tropical illness was a greater foe than enemy bullets.'

R. L. Eichelberger, *Jungle Road to Tokyo* (Odhams Press, 1951)

A detachment of US Marines wade through knee-deep mud on their way to attack Japanese troops on Bougainville, the largest of the Solomon Islands, in November 1943. This was the last major operation of the Solomons campaign.

The Japanese counter-attacked strongly but were defeated in New Georgia in August and the Solomon Islands by October. The Japanese defence of the Solomon Islands cost them 10,000 lives while the Americans lost 1,150 troops. Allied troops then moved to encircle the Japan garrison on Rabaul. By capturing the surrounding islands and constructing air bases on each island they took, they effectively

isolated Rabaul so that it could not be resupplied. By spring 1944 the base had become useless to the Japanese.

The Italian Campaign

In Europe, the Allies now planned to attack the Axis powers by invading Mussolini's Italy. They decided to invade Sicily from Tunisia and use this as a bridgehead to move northwards to occupy the whole of the country.

When the invasion of Italy began in July 1943, the fascist government was already on the verge of economic collapse. Mussolini no longer had popular support, and at the end of July, King Victor Emanuel dismissed him and appointed General Pietro Badoglio. In

US troops wade ashore from their landing craft at the start of the invasion of Salerno, Italy, in September 1943. The Allied commanders believed that the landing would be virtually unopposed, but in fact Field-Marshal Albert Kesselring had time to bring up six divisions, which fiercely resisted the invasion force.

HOW DID IT HAPPEN?

Why was there no second front until 1944?

In April 1942, US Chiefs of Staff adopted proposals for a major invasion of France in spring 1943, but Britain persuaded the USA to drop the plan. A. J. P. Taylor argues that it would not have been possible for the Allies to open a second front before 1944 because the USA and Britain were not yet ready. As seaborne powers they needed to restore their command of the oceans and build more ships before they attempted an invasion of France. Also, careful and lengthy planning for such an operation was required.

However, radical historian Gabriel Kolko argues that Churchill wanted to postpone this second front against Germany in favour of a more indirect policy that favoured Britain in particular – the invasion of North Africa, which would protect British colonial interests in the Mediterranean.

A. J. P. Taylor, *The Second World War* (Hamish Hamilton, 1975); Gabriel Kolko, *The Politics of War* (Pantheon, 1990)

September Badoglio surrendered to the Allies, but Germany was not prepared to give up control of Italy to the Allies, so German forces were sent to invade the country. These forces disarmed the Italian troops in Rome, and the king fled. On the day that Badoglio's surrender was broadcast, the Allies landed in Salerno, southern Italy. The Germans under commander Albert Kesselring engaged them in fierce fighting, and Allied progress northwards proved extremely slow. By the end of 1943, the Allies had still not reached Rome.

While German forces were fully occupied fighting the Allies in Italy and elsewhere, their home country was under attack. The year 1943 marked the height of bombing raids on Germany. US B-17 Flying Fortress bombers operated during daylight and British Bomber Command carried out raids by British planes at night. They attacked the Ruhr, Hamburg and Berlin, with a terrible effect on German cities; thousands of German civilians died and tens of thousands lost their homes. Yet the bombings did not succeed in knocking out weapons factories, so German arms production was little affected.

A B-17 Flying Fortress bomber flies over an industrial target in the area of Cologne, Germany. These bombers were vulnerable to attack by German fighters when they flew beyond the range of their escort of fighter planes. In December 1943, a long-range fighter, the P-51 Mustang, was introduced to protect US B-17 bombers on missions over Germany.

5 Pushing Back the Axis Powers

US general Mark Clark rides through Rome following the liberation of the city in June 1944. Clark commanded the Allied forces during the Italian campaign. Although the conquest of Rome was important symbolically, the German forces were able to retreat and form a new defensive line north of the city.

Despite the setbacks that they had experienced during the year, at the end of 1943 the German and Japanese empires were still largely intact. At the Tehran conference in November 1943, Churchill, Roosevelt and Stalin pledged to work together until they had defeated Germany. They decided that, finally, Allied landings would take place in northern France in 1944.

As plans for the invasion of France were being laid, the Allied campaign in Italy progressed. In January 1944 Allied forces landed at Anzio, south of Rome. The Germans had established the Gustav Line in the mountains just north of Anzio, and the Allies needed to break through it to move northwards. Despite dogged resistance by the Germans, the Allies succeeded in breaking through the Gustav Line in May and by the end of the month, the German defences collapsed. In June a US army marched on Rome, the capital of Italy, which was an important symbolic victory.

D-Day Landings

The conflict in Italy was still not over when the invasion of France took place. The landings in Normandy, in the north-west of the country, were carefully planned. The first day of landings was given the codename D-Day for the unspecified day on which the military attack would be launched. On 5 June, minesweepers cleared a lane through the English Channel and 5,000 vessels followed. That night, to aid the Allies, French Resistance fighters sabotaged rail and communication links in France.

Early on 6 June, Allied ships bombarded German defensive positions in eastern Normandy, and British, Canadian and US soldiers landed on French soil. The fighting was intense, but within a few weeks they began to push back the Germans and to make progress eastwards through France.

By late 1944 Allied forces had freed most of France and Belgium. In December, the troops were marching through Belgium towards Germany, believing that the war was won. They were surprised when the Germans launched a fierce counter-attack at the Battle of Ardennes, popularly known as the Battle of the Bulge, in an attempt to prevent an Allied invasion of Germany. It was unsuccessful, however, and in January 1945 the Germans withdrew.

It was clear after the Battle of Ardennes that Germany was close to defeat. At the start of 1945 the Allies prepared for victory.

This US soldier, keeping watch from a foxhole on a beach in Normandy, was a member of the Allied Expeditionary Force that made the first landings in France on D-Day, 6 June 1944. Above him, a sign in German warns that there are minefields ahead.

VOICES FROM THE PAST

The defender's viewpoint

Franz Gockel, a German soldier whose 18th birthday was on D-Day, described the D-Day attacks from his perspective:

'The opponent wanted to "defeat" us, as it was called in those days, and we did our best in order to repel this opponent, and we did not think about the individual human being. When the landing troops arrived, we said that on every single boat there were more soldiers than in our entire bay of six kilometres. ... this large one [landing boat] which landed right in front of us had about 200-300 men, and they had their exit on both sides, and stood bunched up ... and one comrade who was 50 metres in front of me ... came crawling into my bunker, and shouted, "Franz, beware, they are coming. Now you have to defend yourself." And this is what we both did.'

Quoted on the BBC History website, 2004

During the Yalta conference in February, Roosevelt, Churchill and Stalin discussed how Europe would be ruled after the war and drew up plans for the establishment of the United Nations.

On 12 January 1945, the reconquest of eastern Europe began when Stalin launched an offensive towards Germany from the east. The Soviet troops advanced rapidly. They took Warsaw in Poland and by the end of the month were approaching the German capital, Berlin. On 27 January Soviet troops liberated the prisoners in Auschwitz concentration camp. The emaciated survivors that they discovered among the dead gave a glimpse of the horrors of Hitler's Holocaust.

The leaders of the three main allies (from left): Churchill, Roosevelt and Stalin at the Yalta conference of February 1945.

While the Soviet troops were advancing from the east, the Allies renewed their bombing campaign against Germany. British bombers attacked Dresden in February, for example, killing somewhere between 25,000 and over 100,000 people (estimates vary). The purpose of the campaign was to force German air power to

VOICES FROM THE PAST

The mass bombing of Germany

Although Winston Churchill authorized the bombing of Dresden, apparently he realized afterwards that such drastic action had not been necessary when Germany was on the point of collapse. On 28 March 1945, he wrote to the Chief of Staffs Committee:

'It seems to me that the moment has come when the question of bombing of German cities simply for the sake of increasing the terror, though under other pretexts, should be reviewed. ... Otherwise we may come into control of an utterly ruined land. ... The destruction of Dresden remains a serious query against the conduct of Allied bombing.'

Even after the war, Sir Arthur Harris, head of RAF Bomber Command, continued to believe that the area bombing of Germany had helped to end the war although many British people condemned it as an unnecessary action:

'In spite of all that happened at Hamburg, bombing proved a comparatively humane method. For one thing, it saved the youth of this country and of our allies from being mown down by the military as it was in the war of 1914–1918.'

Churchill quoted in *Socialist Review*, UK (February 1995); Sir Arthur Harris, writing in his memoirs, *Bomber Offensive* (Greenhill Books, 1947)

Opposite below: Street fighting took place in Berlin as Soviet forces fought to gain control of Germany's capital in April 1945. Stalin wanted his Soviet forces to reach Berlin before the other Allies who were approaching from the west, and he deployed two million men in the advance on the city.

concentrate on the defence of the homeland and to divert workers from arms production to essential repair work.

The Soviet forces pressed on towards Germany from the east, while the Western Allies moved in from the south and west. Soviet troops pushed the Germans out of Budapest, Hungary in February, out of Czechoslovakia in March, and out of Vienna in April. On 16 April they attacked Berlin and by the 29th Hitler knew he had lost the war. Meanwhile, British, US, Canadian and French forces advanced through Italy, and on 29 April the German forces there capitulated. The following day Hitler committed suicide in his bunker in the ruins of Berlin and on 7 May Germany surrendered. On 8 May Victory in Europe Day – VE Day – was celebrated.

During 1944, as Germany was nearing defeat, Japan's empire was also pushed back. Since the Battle of Midway Japan had been experiencing serious fuel shortages and could not produce sufficient new ships and aircraft to make up for its losses.

Nevertheless, in spring 1944 Japanese forces were still on the march. They extended their control in China, moving into the interior of the country. The Chinese armies were not able to mount successful resistance. However, the Allies decided that China was no longer an important theatre of conflict; they would defeat Japan in other areas, such as Burma, Saipan and the Philippines.

Burma and Saipan

The USA wanted the British to attack the Japanese forces that occupied Burma in order to reopen the Burma road. The Japanese were determined to defend it. They struck first, but their offensive failed, and the British were able to advance into Burma.

US Marines landed on the beach on Saipan in June 1944. The USA assembled huge forces, as did the Japanese, who had foreseen the attack and were therefore not taken by surprise. Before the action began, the message of the Japanese admiral to his fleet was 'The fate of the empire rests on this one battle.'

In June, the Americans invaded Saipan in the Mariana Islands, a vital stronghold in the outer defences of Japan's territory. If Saipan was breached, Japan's national defences would no longer be effective as its capture brought Japan within range of US B-29 bombers. The battle was a disaster for Japan, which lost nearly 400 aircraft and thousands of men. The fall of Saipan was a severe setback for the Japanese military and political command. Prime minister General Tojo Hideki resigned over this failure and was replaced by General Koiso Kuniaki.

The USA now swept through the Pacific and captured the strongholds of Tinian and Guam in August. In October, MacArthur launched an attack on the Philippines, which ended with the conquest of the capital, Manila, in March 1945.

However, the US conquest of the Pacific was not without obstacles. When the Americans attacked Iwo Jima in February and Okinawa at the start of April, they met with stiff resistance from the Japanese. The battles on Okinawa lasted for almost three months. The Japanese defended their positions using kamikaze forces – volunteer suicide pilots who flew their aircraft to crash on the decks of ships and explode. Japan's forces suffered enormous casualties, though; by the time the Americans had conquered Okinawa, over one hundred thousand Japanese had died.

HOW DID IT HAPPEN?

How crucial was D-Day to the Allied victory?

Every 6 June, the countries that fought Germany commemorate D-Day. Second World War specialist Martin Gilbert argues that failure in Normandy could have allowed Hitler to continue to rule western Europe, particularly if the United States had turned all its energies to the ever-growing demands of the Pacific war. Military historian Professor Richard Holmes, however, believes that the importance of D-Day is overemphasized. Brave though the fighters were, there were broader reasons for the Allied victory. Without the Allied navies keeping the sea lanes open, the destruction of the *Luftwaffe* by Allied air forces and the Soviet victories on the Eastern Front, it is unlikely that the D-Day invasion would have succeeded.

Martin Gilbert, *Turning Points in History: D-Day* (Wiley, 2004); Richard Holmes, 'The 'D-Day Dodgers', BBC History website, 2004

This huge hole in the deck of the US aircraft carrier, USS *Bunker Hill*, was caused by the impact of two kamikaze planes near Okinawa, Japan in May 1945. The attack left 346 men dead, 43 missing and 264 wounded. The kamikaze pilots who carried out such suicide attacks were genuine volunteers, although the US forces found it hard to believe that they had not been conscripted.

6 The End of the War and Its Aftermath

This photograph shows the industrial area of Tokyo, flattened by US bombing in March 1945. Rather than aiming at specific targets, the US air force used incendiary bombs that created firestorms and caused huge devastation over a wide area. About 100,000 people died – more than in either of the atomic bomb attacks of the following August.

In spring 1945 Japan was close to collapse. Many factories could no longer operate because they had no coal or raw materials, and two-thirds of Japanese ships had been sunk. US bombers attacked Japan from the air. In one raid on Tokyo on 8 March, 83,000 people were killed. (By comparison, 60,000 British civilians were killed in air attacks during the entire war.)

In May 1945 the British forces drove the Japanese out of Burma. The new Japanese prime minister, Baron Suzuki Kantaro, called on Stalin to act as an intermediary in order to help negotiate Japan's surrender but Stalin felt that the Japanese approach to peace was too vague and refused the request. Then in July, the Allies at the Potsdam

VOICES FROM THE PAST

The writing on the wall

Kase Toshikazu, a senior Japanese Foreign Ministry official, was pro-British and pro-American; after the fall of Saipan, he worked to secure peace with the Allies. In early 1944 he wrote in his diary:

'Defeat now stares us stark in the face. There is only one question left: how can we avert the chaos attendant upon a disastrous defeat? The preservation of my fatherland, that is a paramount [most important] task assigned to me by fate. The hostile attack is developing so surprisingly swiftly that it may be that diplomacy cannot intervene before it is too late. I must redouble my efforts to expedite [speed up] the restoration of peace.'

Quoted in Peter Calvocoressi, Guy Wint and John Pritchard, *The Penguin History of the Second World War* (Penguin, 1989)

conference called upon Japan to capitulate. Suzuki did not give a direct reply, and the Americans believed that he had treated their call with contempt. The war continued.

Hiroshima and Nagasaki

Stalin was prepared to become involved in the Far East to secure Japan's defeat. But US leaders wanted to prevent Soviet intervention, which might lead to an extension of the USSR's influence in the region. Instead, President Harry Truman (who had recently succeeded Roosevelt upon the latter's death in April 1945) decided to use atomic bombs to force Japan to surrender. Not all senior US figures agreed with this decision. General Dwight Eisenhower, who had commanded the Allied forces in Europe, said later that he believed 'it wasn't necessary to hit them with that awful thing'.

On 6 August, the Americans dropped the world's first atomic bomb on the Japanese city of Hiroshima. Three days later, another bomb was dropped on Nagasaki. The effects of the atomic bombs were devastating. About 110,000 died instantly as the bombs exploded. The bombs flattened the two cities and unleashed atomic radiation over a wide area. Thousands more people later died from wounds, burns or leukaemia caused by radiation. Following

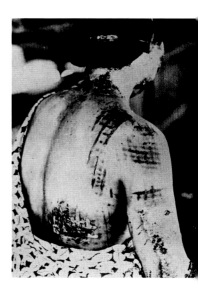

This woman was seriously injured during the atomic bomb explosion that devastated Hiroshima on 6 August 1945. The pattern of the kimono she was wearing at the time of the explosion is burnt into her skin. Nearly all the survivors within about half a kilometre of the blast later died a slow death from the effects of radiation.

About 60 million people were displaced from their homes during the Second World War. Many did not want to return home afterwards; for example, a large number were unhappy about returning to Communist rule. These refugees from Lodz, Poland, which had been liberated by the USSR, hoped to reach the British sector of Berlin.

the attacks, on 14 August Japan agreed to surrender. The Second World War was over.

The costs of the Second World War were vast. Out of 70 million combatants, 17 million died. The Soviet forces lost the largest proportion of their fighters – 1 in 22, and the Americans the least – 1 in 500. Even more civilians lost their lives: up to 20 million in the USSR and perhaps 4.5 million in Germany. Civilians died in air raids, from forced labour or starvation under siege, or they were deliberately murdered by the Nazis. Poland lost perhaps 20 percent of its population, the USSR 10 percent. Japanese casualties were about 2 million, while deaths in China numbered somewhere between 2.5 and 13.5 million. The Nazis murdered about 6 million of Europe's 9 million Jews and virtually wiped out the Roma of eastern Europe.

Many countries were ravaged by war. Soviet Russia suffered the greatest loss: 1,710 towns and 70,000 villages had been destroyed. Vast areas of land were laid waste, left completely bare and uninhabited. Germany was also war-torn; the city of Hamburg alone suffered more damage than the whole of Britain, although the country's industrial resources were not seriously affected. Most Japanese cities lay in ruins. The industrial resources of Poland and France were halved. In Britain, 500,000 homes were destroyed. The USA was the only country that emerged economically stronger from the war.

VOICES FROM THE PAST

Charter of the United Nations

In order to try to prevent future conflicts, in October 1945, the USA, Britain and the USSR took the lead in the establishing the United Nations, an international organization that would aim to preserve world peace. Its aims were summarized in its charter:

We the peoples of the United Nations [are] determined
to save succeeding generations from the scourge of war,
which twice in our lifetime has brought untold sorrow to
mankind, and

to reaffirm faith in fundamental human rights, in the dignity
and worth of the human person, in the equal rights of men and
women and of nations large and small, and

to establish conditions under which justice and respect for
the obligations arising from treaties and other sources of
international law can be maintained, and

to promote social progress and better standards of life in
larger freedom...

Preamble to the UN Charter, June 1945

This street barricade was located between the American and the Soviet zones of Berlin that were established after the war. The division of Germany in 1945 put Berlin within East Germany. However, the city itself was divided into two sections: West Berlin, which was part of the Federal Republic of Germany, and East Berlin, which became the capital of East Germany.

Making Peace

Amid the devastation of war, the Allies discussed peace treaties at the Potsdam conference in Germany during July–August 1945, but no agreement was reached until the following year. The Allies finally signed peace treaties with Bulgaria, Finland, Hungary, Italy and Romania in 1947. It was decided that France, Britain, the USSR and the USA would share control of Germany, and that each power could seize reparations from its occupation zone. The Soviet zone became the Communist state of East Germany in 1949, while the Western Allies merged their zones and created the Federal Republic of Germany, which allied with the West. The Americans finally made peace with Japan in 1952.

YOU ARE LEAVING THE AMERICAN SECTOR

ВЫ ВЫЕЗЖАЕТЕ ИЗ АМЕРИКАНСКОЙ ЗОНЫ

VOUS SORTEZ DU SECTEUR AMÉRICAIN

SIE VERLASSEN DEN AMERIKANISCHEN SEKTOR

HOW DID IT HAPPEN?

Was it right to use atomic bombs?

In 1945 and in the years immediately afterwards, the official US view was that the use of atomic bombs was necessary to end the war quickly. An invasion of Japan would have proven lengthy and have cost the Allies a million casualties. Some historians today, such as Robert James Maddox, agree with this analysis. However, J. Samuel Walker, chief historian of the US Nuclear Regulatory Commission, reviewed the recent research in 1990: 'Careful scholarly treatment of the records and manuscripts opened over the past few years has greatly enhanced our understanding of why the Truman administration used atomic weapons against Japan. Experts continue to disagree on some issues, but critical questions have been answered. The consensus among scholars is that the bomb was not needed to avoid an invasion of Japan and to end the war within a relatively short time. It is clear that alternatives to the bomb existed and that Truman and his advisers knew it.' Military specialists today argue that Japan would have surrendered without either an invasion or the dropping of atomic bombs.

Robert James Maddox, *Weapons for Victory: The Hiroshima Decision Fifty Years Later* (University of Missouri Press, 1995); J. Samuel Walker, 'The Decision to Use the Bomb: A Historiographical Update', *Diplomatic History 14* (Winter 1990)

Former Japanese prime minister Tojo Hideki testifies in his own defence during the International Tribunal for Far East war crimes trial in Tokyo in 1947. As a result of the trial, Tojo was convicted and executed.

As well as securing peace treaties, the victors in the war – the USA, Britain, France and the USSR – deemed it necessary to punish the people whom they believed were responsible for the conflict. They established an International Tribunal and brought alleged war criminals to trial. At the Nuremberg Trials of 1945-46, twenty-one German leaders were charged with war crimes; eleven received the death sentence. In a similar trial in Japan, twenty-five leaders were sentenced, of whom eleven were hanged.

Political Developments

The war also brought political changes. In the Far East, the British and the French regained their colonies, albeit temporarily – many

Asian countries gained their independence in the following years. The USA established trusteeship over important strategic islands in the Pacific. The Japanese Empire was disbanded and a new political system created that did not permit the development of military power. The Western powers withdrew their involvement in China, and in 1949 it became a Communist state.

The biggest political development was the creation of two new superpowers in the world: the USSR and the USA. From 1945, the USSR set up Communist governments in the eastern European countries it had conquered during the final phase of the war. The USA, which had provided financial backing for its allies during the war, had become the strongest country economically and now exerted tremendous influence around the globe.

The two former Allies became enemies. In March 1946, Winston Churchill said in a speech in Fulton, Missouri: 'From Stettin in the Baltic, to Trieste, in the Adriatic, an iron curtain has descended across the [European] continent. Behind that curtain…all are subject to Soviet influence and a very high degree of control from Moscow [the Soviet capital].' This speech is generally said to mark the start of Cold War, a struggle for influence in the world between the superpowers without direct military action. In March 1947, Truman declared that the USA would support other countries to stop them from becoming Communist. The world became divided once again – this time between the Communist sphere and the USA and its allies – a division that was to last for nearly half a century.

Russian and American troops meet at the River Elbe in Torgau, Germany, during the final stages of the Allied invasion of Germany in April 1945. Once their common enemies had been defeated, the co-operation that existed during the war between the USSR and the USA proved to be short-lived.

Second World War Timeline

1937 War breaks out between China and Japan

1938
12 March: Hitler incorporates Austria into Germany
29 September: The Munich Agreement: Czechoslovakia cedes land to Germany, Hungary and Poland

1939
15 March: Nazi forces occupy all of Czechoslovakia
22 May: Hitler and Mussolini form an alliance, the Pact of Steel
23 August: Nazi-Soviet Non-Aggression Pact between Germany and the USSR
1 September: Hitler invades Poland; Britain and France declare war

1940
9 April: Germany invades Denmark and Norway
10 May: Germany invades the Netherlands, Belgium, Luxembourg and France
10 June: Mussolini declares war on the Allies
June: Battle of the Atlantic starts
July-October: The Battle of Britain
3 August: Italian forces advance into British Somaliland
23 August: The Blitz begins
27 September: Tripartite Pact between Japan, Italy and Germany

1941
24 March: Rommel's forces mount first attacks in North Africa
22 June: Germany invades the USSR
7 December: Japan attacks the USA at Pearl Harbor. The USA and Britain declare war on Japan; Germany and Italy declare war on the USA
8 December: Japan starts invasions of south-east Asian countries
December: Nazis begin to set up death camps for the Jews

1942
4-7 June: Battle of Midway
21 June: Germans take Tobruk and advance into Egypt
23 October: Start of second Battle of El Alamein
8 November: Allies begin invasion of north-west Africa

1943
7 February: US forces complete the defeat of the Japanese at Guadalcanal
13 May: The Germans surrender in North Africa
20 June: US forces land on New Georgia
5-12 July: Soviet forces defeat the Germans at the Battle of Kursk, Russia

10 July: Allies invade Sicily
2 November: USA conquers the Solomon Islands

1944
22 January: Allied forces land in Anzio, Italy
6 June: Allied D-Day landings in northern France
9 July: Fall of Saipan (Mariana Islands) to the USA
24 August: Liberation of Paris by Allied troops

1945
16 January: Allies defeat Germans in the Ardennes
January: Soviet forces advance towards Germany
28 February: US forces conquer Manila, capital of the Philippines
1 April: US troops land on Okinawa
28 April: Mussolini is killed by Italian partisans
29 April: German forces capitulate in Italy
30 April: Hitler commits suicide in his Berlin bunker
2 May: German troops surrender in Berlin
3 May: British capture Rangoon, Burma from the Japanese
4 May: Germany surrenders
6 and 9 August: USA drops atomic bombs on Hiroshima and Nagasaki
2 September: Japan surrenders
24 October: The United Nations is established

Glossary

appeasement The policy of offering concessions to an aggressor in an attempt to prevent conflict.

atomic bomb A nuclear weapon with violent explosive power that destroys everything in the range of the explosion and releases radiation into the atmosphere.

collaborate To co-operate with or willingly assist an enemy of one's country, especially an occupying force.

Communist Someone who believes in Communism, a political system in which the state's property is owned by the people and where the country's wealth is shared equally amongst all workers.

concentration camp A prison camp set up by the Nazis for the detention of political prisoners and people that they saw as enemies, especially the

Jews. Prisoners were often worked to death but not deliberately murdered.

conscription Compulsory military service.

convoy A group of ships travelling together with military protection.

coup A violent or illegal seizure of power.

death camps Camps in Poland where Jews and other minority groups were taken to be killed.

embargo An order by a state to stop trade.

ghetto Enclosed and guarded area of a town or city where Jews under Nazi occupation were forced to live.

Lebensraum Means 'living space'; the term used by the Nazis to justify their claim to large areas of eastern Europe, land which they said was needed to provide space for

the German population.

nationalist movement Movement of people that believe that the inhabitants of a certain territory share loyalty to a nation.

reparations Compensation for war damage that is paid by the defeated state to the victors.

Resistance General term for the underground movements formed in Europe to resist the Nazi occupation.

Roma A traditionally nomadic people originally from India, who mostly lived in Europe.

sabotage Deliberate damage to production or transport.

sanctions Military or economic action by a state to try to force another to comply with its wishes or with an international agreement.

tribunal A court of justice.

trusteeship Supervisory control by a country over a territory.

Further Information

Books:

Adams, Simon, *DK Eyewitness Books: World War II* (DK Publishing Inc., 2004)

Goldstein, Margaret, *Chronicle of America's Wars: World War II* (Lerner Publications, 2004)

Grant, Reg, *World War II: Europe* (Franklin Watts, 2004)

Hatt, Christine, *Documenting History: World War II* (Franklin Watts, 2001)

Nardo, Don, *Opposing Viewpoints in World History: World War II* (Greenhaven Press, 2005)

Gavin, Philip, *World History: World War II in Europe* (Lucent Books, 2004)

Sheehan, Sean, *World War II: The Pacific* (Franklin Watts, 2004)

Wills, Charles, *Battles and Leaders: World War II* (DK Publishing Inc., 2004)

Websites:

http://en.wikipedia.org/wiki/World_war_II

http://library.thinkquest.org/18106/overview. html?tqskip1=1

http://www.bbc.co.uk/history/war/wwtwo/ index.shtml

http://www.spartacus.schoolnet.co.uk/2WWchron. htm

Index   Numbers in **bold** refer to pictures